MY BEST BOOK OF

ROCKS

AND FOSSILS

Chris Pellant

KINGFISHER

LONDON & NEW YORK

KINGFISHER
LONDON & NEW YORK

Copyright © Macmillan Children's Books 2000, 2007, 2019
First published 2000 in the United States by Kingfisher
This edition published 2019 by Kingfisher
120 Broadway, New York, NY 10271
Kingfisher is an imprint of Macmillan Children's Books, London
All rights reserved.

Distributed in the U.S. and Canada by Macmillan,
120 Broadway, New York, NY 10271

Library of Congress Cataloging-in-Publication data has
been applied for.

ISBN 978-0-7534-7526-3

Design by Wildpixel Ltd.
Illustrations: Ray Grinaway, Chris Forsey

Kingfisher books are available for special promotions and
premiums. For details contact: Special Markets Department,
Macmillan, 120 Broadway, New York, NY 10271

For more information please visit:
www.kingfisherbooks.com

Printed in China
10 9 8 7 6 5 4 3 2 1
1TR/0719/WKT/UNTD/128MA

The Publisher would like to thank the following for permission to
reproduce their material.
Top = t; Bottom = b; Center = c; Left = l; Right = r
1 loonger.iStock; 4 NASA Images/Shutterstock; 6-7 Daniel Prudek/
Shutterstock; 6 Realest Nature/Shutterstock; 7t sandatlas.org/
Shutterstock; 7b Richard Bradford/Shutterstock; 8-9 Anton Foltin/
Shutterstock; 9t Lmspencer/Shutterstock; 9b Creative Travel Projects/
Shutterstock; 10-11 ConradFries/iStock; 10 Sebastian Janicki/
Shutterstock; 12-13 arkanto/Shutterstock; 12cl electra/Shutterstock;
12br BorneoJC James/Shutterstock; 12br maxpetrov/Shutterstock;
12cr Yulia Grigoryeva/Shutterstock; 13tl Interfoto/Alamy Stock Photo;
14-15 Chaay_Tea/Shutterstock; 14 Max Mumby/Indigi/Getty Images;
15br Ileysen/Shutterstock; 16-17 Kues/Shutterstock; 17tr Marcio Jose
Bastos Silva/Shutterstock; 17cl Bjoern Wylezich/Shutterstock; 17br
alice-photo/Shutterstock; 17bl footageclips/Shutterstock; 18-19bg
Dmitry Polonskiy/Shutterstock; 19cr Maderia/Shutterstock; 19cl Andrew
Hayes/Alamy Stock Photo; 20-21 Dariusz Leszczynski/Shutterstock;
20 Warpaint/Shutterstock; 21t Akkharat Jarusilawong/Shutterstock;
21cl Harschel Hoffmeyer/Shutterstock; 21bl Elenarts/Shutterstock;
22 sisqopote/Shutterstock; 22-23 WavyBxl/Shutter; 24-25 c iurii/
Shutterstock; 25tc snapinadil/Shutterstock; 26-27 Bas van der Plujim/
Shutterstock; 26 Tom Grundy/Shutterstock; 27 jonnysek/iStock; 28-29
Vadim Sadovski/Shutterstock; 28b RomoloTavani iStock; 30-31 Ferita
Rahayuningsih/Shutterstock; 32 loonger iStock.

CONTENTS

THE AGE OF EARTH

Our rocky planet is older than we could ever imagine. Around 4,600 million years ago, Earth was a huge, fiery ball circling the Sun. Much of the surface was covered with hot, liquid rock—lava that poured out from volcanoes and meteorites that had crashed down from space.

crust

mantle

solid core

liquid core

Under our feet

Earth has a hard rocky crust. Below the crust lies the mantle, which is so hot that in some places the rock has melted. The core is even hotter and is made of both solid and liquid metal.

Cooling down

Over millions of years, Earth's surface began to cool and shrink. Inside of Earth, chemical substances called minerals joined together to make different kinds of rocks. A rocky crust formed on the outside. Today, Earth's surface seems solid, but new rocks are constantly forming.

OUR ROCKY WORLD

The rocks that we see today on Earth's surface are formed in different ways. Geologists have discovered that all rocks belong to three main groups: sedimentary, igneous, and metamorphic. The names describe how the rocks were made—sedimentary means "made from sediment," igneous means "fiery," and metamorphic means "changed."

Made by fire

Many igneous rocks form when lava is forced out of an erupting volcano and then cools and hardens on the surface.

Layers of sediment

Sedimentary rocks are made from sediments such as sand, clay, and seashells that pile up in layers in lakes, rivers, and oceans. Over time these layers are pressed tightly together to make solid rock.

Changed rocks

Metamorphic rocks form in the ground when heat and pressure change the structure and appearance of igneous and sedimentary rocks. The changed rocks are pushed up from under the ground to form hills and mountains.

NATURE'S BEAUTY

Earth has many beautiful hills and dramatic landscapes. Every valley, hill, and mountain is carved out of rock. Yet landscapes change constantly as rivers, glaciers, and the sea wear away the rocks.

Deep valley

Over thousands of years the rushing waters of the Colorado River have cut through rock to form the Grand Canyon. Layers of sedimentary rock can clearly be seen running along the sides of the canyon.

Giant steps

Giant's Causeway in Northern Ireland is made from igneous rock. As the volcanic rock cooled, it shrank and cracked to form thousands of six-sided columns. The rocks look like a giant staircase leading down to the sea.

Mighty peaks

The Alps are a high, rugged mountain range in Europe. These soaring peaks are made from metamorphic rock that was first forced to the surface 30 million years ago. In geological terms these mountains are still very young.

MINERALS AND CRYSTALS

Minerals are the natural elements and compounds in the Earth's crust that make up rocks. There are more than 3,800 different minerals, and many form beautiful crystals. Gemstones, salts, metals such as gold, and even talc are all different types of minerals. Geologists identify minerals by looking at features like color, shape, and hardness.

Crystal creation

Hot liquids rich in minerals move through Earth's crust. As these liquids cool, the minerals grow into crystals in hollows in rocks.

This amethyst has large, six-sided crystals

Color

A good way of identifying minerals is to study their color, which can be one of their most striking features. They come in a range of bright and vivid colors.

Shape

When crystals grow, they make many wonderful shapes. The shapes are the result of the neat arrangement of atoms and molecules inside the mineral.

Hardness

Each mineral has a certain hardness that is measured by how easily it is scratched by another object. The softest mineral is talc, and the hardest is diamond.

Azurite has blue crystals

Barite has flat oblongs

Malachite has green crystals

Hematite is kidney-shaped

Realgar has red crystals

Diamond cannot be scratched by any other object

Galena has gray crystals

Fluorite can be scratched with a blade

Quartz is hexagon-shaped

Calcite can be scratched with a coin

Pyrite is cube-shaped

Talc can be scratched with a fingernail

MINERALS AT WORK

Throughout history, people have dug up minerals and rocks from the ground and used them to make many everyday objects. The discovery of metals and other raw materials changed the way people lived. Valuable metals, called ores, were found in rocks. Many items can be made by using mixtures of metals, or alloys.

The aluminum can story

1. Aluminum is a light, easily shaped metal. It comes from an ore called bauxite, which is dug out of huge quarries. The ore is then taken to a refining factory to remove the metal.

2. In order to remove the aluminum from the ore, the raw bauxite is heated beyond its melting point. This is called smelting. The melted aluminum is made into flat sheets of metal.

3. At another factory, the aluminum goes through further changes. Gradually, the sheets of metal are made into thousands of small cans that are used for holding drinks and food.

4. Earth contains enough bauxite to last for the next 300 years. However, melting down scrap aluminum is much cheaper than mining it. Collect and recycle as many used cans as possible.

Ancient alloy

Bronze is a mixture of tin and copper. It is strong and hard-wearing.

Roman metal

The Romans used lead for making their water pipes because it was very easy to bend. They heated the ore to extract the pure metal.

Renaissance color

During the Renaissance, painters crushed up brightly colored minerals to make pigments. They mixed these with oil to make paints.

Writing material

When we write with a pencil, we are using a mineral. The thin, black material in a pencil is called graphite.

PRECIOUS GEMSTONES

Gemstones are formed from minerals inside Earth's crust. When rough gems are cut and polished, they become very beautiful and valuable objects. For thousands of years people have worn gems because of their amazing color, special shape, and dazzling beauty. Some of the rarest and most precious jewels are diamonds, rubies, sapphires, and emeralds.

Royal jewels

There are more than 3,000 precious gemstones set in the British Imperial State Crown, including 2,868 diamonds. The crown also contains 4 rubies, 11 green emeralds, 17 blue sapphires, and 269 shiny pearls. It is very heavy—it weighs more than two pounds.

The Imperial Sate Crown is part of the British crown jewels. It is worn by the queen, Elizabeth II, for special royal events.

In the raw

Gems found in rocks look a little dull in their natural state. Experts cut them out of the rock and then shape and polish them until they sparkle and shine.

Gemstone in rock

Rough gemstone

Glittering jewel

Birthstones

People sometimes wear a special gemstone called a birthstone in a piece of jewelry. The stone shows in what month of the year a person was born. People also believe that birthstones bring good luck to the wearer.

Garnet
January

Diamond
April

Ruby
July

Opal
October

Amethyst
February

Emerald
May

Peridot
August

Topaz
November

Aquamarine
March

Pearl
June

Sapphire
September

Turquoise
December

FaSCINaTINg FOSSILS

Fossils are the remains, or traces, of long-dead animals and plants and can be millions of years old. Most fossils are discovered in sedimentary rock in areas that were once in or near water such as seas or rivers. They were formed after prehistoric plants and animals died and were buried under layers of sediment. While the soft parts rotted away, the hard parts, such as shells, bones, teeth, and even whole skeletons, became fossils.

How fossils form

1. When a fish dies, its body sinks to the seabed. The soft parts of the fish rot away.

2. Gradually, the skeleton is covered with layers of sand and mud. This settles and becomes solid rock.

3. After millions of years, movements inside Earth bring the rocks containing the fossil above sea level.

4. The rocks containing the fossil are worn away by the weather and the fossil is exposed on land.

Frozen in time

Not all fossils are found in stone. Some plants and animals are found as they were in life. There are many different ways in which fossils can be preserved.

This detailed fossil of an early fish has been preserved in stone.

Insects can be preserved whole in pine tree resin. Over time, this turns into amber.

Ice can preserve bodies. This baby mammoth was found frozen in the ice in Siberia, in Russia.

The wood of this tree trunk has been replaced, molecule by molecule, by minerals that turned to stone. This is called petrification.

This ancient leaf imprint is almost 300 million years old. The original leaf was fossilized in layers of coal.

LAYERS OF LIFE

Millions of living things have existed on Earth, but only a small number of them became fossils. Fossils are very important because they show how life on our planet has changed over many millions of years.

one million years ago
1. Early elephant

100 million years ago
2. Flesh-eating dinosaur

200 million years ago
3. Early reptile
4. Ammonite

300 million years a
5. Early amphibian
6. Horsetail plant

Over the past 600 million years, life-forms have changed from simple, soft-bodied creatures, through fish and reptiles to the advanced animals that exist today.

Trace fossils

Fossils that show where animals have been are called trace fossils. Many large dinosaurs left fossilized footprints and eggs as evidence of where they once lived.

Dinosaur eggs

Dinosaur footprint in the rock

Dating Earth

Earth's history is divided into periods. Different creatures and plants lived at different times. Geologists can tell how old rocks are by studying the kinds of fossils that are found in them.

400 million years ago
7. Cephalaspis
8. Early fish

500 million years ago
9. Brachiopod
10. Trilobite

600 million years ago
11. Ediacaran animal

10

11

CLUES TO THE PAST

Evolution is the way in which animals and plants change over many generations. Fossils are clues about how life on Earth has evolved. They show us the links between many of today's species and their long-extinct ancestors. For example, by studying the *Archaeopteryx* fossils found in Germany, scientists discovered more about the ancient link between birds and reptiles.

Clawed climber

Archaeopteryx spent much of its time in trees using the sharp claws on its feet and wings to climb.

Missing link

In 1861 the discovery of the first *Archaeopteryx* fossil amazed scientists. They believed that it was the remains of a bird because it had feathers and wings. But it also had some reptilelike features such as sharp teeth, claws, scaly legs, and a long, bony tail. For the first time, a possible link between reptiles and birds had been found.

Archaeopteryx had razor-like teeth, ideal for eating prey like dragonflies.

Winged wonder

Archaeopteryx was a poor flier and would have used its wide wings to glide from branch to branch or to swoop to the ground.

FOSSIL HUNTERS

Discovering a new dinosaur site is an exciting event. The remains of these creatures have been found in remote places as far apart as the United States, China, Australia, and Great Britain. Occasionally, people have stumbled across dinosaur bones by accident. More often, the bones are found by geologists who know where to look.

Dinosaur dig

When a skeleton is unearthed, it has to be moved carefully because the bones are very fragile. The remains are then taken to a museum to be studied and put on display.

A brush is used to remove dust and sand from around the fossil.

She sells seashells

This tongue twister is about Mary Anning, a young English fossil hunter. Early in the 1800s she discovered the skeleton of an ichthyosaur near the sea in England. This was one of the first fossils of this marine reptile ever to be found, and she sold it for a large amount of money.

Rock is carefully removed from around the skeleton using special tools.

rOSSIL rUELS

Coal, oil, and natural gas are all fossil fuels and supply most of the energy we use to power our cars, homes, and schools. They are formed from ancient plants and animals and are found in underground rocks. Coal is made from fossilized plants while oil is made from the remains of tiny sea creatures that lived millions of years ago.

How coal forms

1. Millions of years ago, huge swampy forests covered Earth. As the giant trees and plants died, they fell onto the wet forest floor. They were covered by mud and began to rot.

2. Gradually, the plant remains were buried under more layers of rock and mud. Over millions of years they turned into peat, and eventually into hard, black coal.

3. The coal lies in deep, underground seams. To reach it, a shaft is dug down to the layer of coal. A horizontal tunnel is drilled along the seam, and the coal is brought to the surface.

Workers access the
oil rig by helicopter

Excess gas
burning off

Oil rig

An oil rig is a platform
attached to the seabed
that drills into the rocks
below and pumps up
the oil. The oil is then
sent down the pipelines
to land where it is made
into gasoline and other
products.

Stabilizing leg
attached to the seabed

STARTING A COLLECTION

The best way to learn about fossils, rocks, and minerals is to start your own collection. Keep an eye out for new specimens near beaches, cliffs, and other places where rocks are exposed. Try to find an interesting rock in every place you visit.

Eager explorers

Beaches are great places to hunt for rocks and fossils. Fossils are exposed as the wind and waves wash away soil and plants and break up the rocks. Do not damage or disturb the sites you visit and don't take too many fossils. Always leave something of interest for other collectors to find. Remember to tell an adult before you go collecting.

Displaying

Once you have found some interesting rocks and fossils, clean them carefully. It is very important to make a list of the fossils you have found and where you found them. Try identifying any new finds by looking them up in a book. You can read about their history and label them with the correct names. You can put the best ones on display.

OUT OF THIS WORLD

Look up into the clear night sky and you may be able to see bright sparks of light flying across it. These are called shooting stars and are caused by meteoroids, which are lumps of space rock left over from the birth of other planets in the solar system.

Mighty meteorites

When meteoroids enter Earth's atmosphere, they burn up in the intense heat and glow brightly. The lumps that actually reach Earth's surface are called meteorites. Although they are extremely rare, some do strike our planet every year. Many of them crash into the oceans or remote areas like deserts.

Lunar landscapes

Moon rocks collected by astronauts have provided scientists with clues about the Moon's history. Tests show that the Moon's rocks are similar to rocks found all over Earth. Because of this, scientists now think that the Moon may once have been part of Earth.

An astronaut scoops up rock samples from the surface of the Moon

Anorthosite

Basalt

Breccia

UNEARTHING THE FACTS

As your collection of fossils, rocks, and minerals grows, you will want to find out more. Try looking in your local library for useful books or ask your science teacher for information. If you visit a natural history museum, there should be a collection of interesting fossils, rocks, and minerals, as well as people who can help you identify your own specimens. The more you study Earth, the more you realize that it is a beautiful place full of natural treasures that must all be carefully protected.

With 60 razor-sharp teeth, the *Tyrannosaurus* is one of the most feared animals of all time.

Dinosaur displays

Dinosaurs are often the most popular part of a museum exhibition, like this *Tyrannosaurus* skeleton. Scientists can learn a lot about how these creatures lived by studying their remains. Someone who studies fossils is called a paleontologist.

GLOSSARY

alloy A mixture of metals, or of a metal and another substance.

basalt An igneous rock that forms from hardened lava after a volcanic eruption.

bauxite The rock ore from which aluminum is refined.

bronze An alloy made from copper and tin.

canyon A very deep, narrow valley, often formed when a river cuts through rock.

compound Two or more elements joined together chemically.

core The center of Earth, made of heavy metals.

crust The outer, rocky layer of Earth.

crystal The special shape in which many minerals form. A crystal has fixed properties and the sides are usually flat and regular.

dinosaurs The group of now extinct reptiles that lived between 230 and 65 million years ago.

evolution The way in which organisms change over time. Simple life-forms have evolved into complex animals and plants.

fossil The remains, or traces, of animals and plants usually preserved in rocks.

fossil fuels The fuels coal, oil, and natural gas, all of which are formed from the remains of once-living organisms.

gemstone A mineral that is valuable because of its beauty, often worn in a piece of jewelry.

geologist Someone who studies rocks and fossils to learn about Earth's history.

graphite A mineral made entirely of the element carbon. Graphite is very soft and black.

lava The hot, melted rock that pours out of an erupting volcano.

magma The hot, liquid rock deep in Earth's crust that becomes lava on the surface.

meteorite A lump of rock from outer space that hits Earth's surface.

mineral A compound or an element that forms crystals. All rocks are made from minerals.

ore A mineral that contains valuable material such as metal.

petrification The process of being turned to stone.

resin The sticky liquid that oozes from pine trees and hardens to form amber.

rock A mass of mineral material that may or may not be solid.

smelting The process by which a metal is removed from an ore.

INDEX